BASED ON TRUE EVENTS

DECEPTION

ANITA RILEY

Published by Lee's Press and Publishing Company
www.LeesPress.net

A Premiere Self-Publishing
Services Company

ISBN-13: 979-8-9896434-6-2

PAPERBACK

DEDICATION

This book is dedicated to my two son's Ernest Riley Jr., Elonte Riley, my dear granddaughter Ya'niya Riley who is very dear to my heart and the First Harvest Faith Christian Center members Min. Ozie Felder, Min. Gillis Sloan, Evan Betty Anthony, Dea. Al Fairly, Sis. Lynn Johnson and Ralph Watkins. (Just to name a few.) I like to thank you for pushing me when I thought I couldn't go on.

INTRODUCTION

This book was written to let people know about the deception that's going on in the world and how the Enemy has deceived so many people. It is so hard even to turn on the News, read the newspaper and the internet without hearing something that is not true. It is so many lies going on that it is unreal. This world was created by God. We stood on the word of God, but now everyone wants to take God out of the equation. People are making the wrong right and the right wrong. As you read this book, we will find what God has to say about this. People, wake up, get your life in order. God is watching. The scriptures are real; the people are made up.

DECEPTION - THE STORY

What does the Bible have to say about deceit or deception? It's only a (6) six or a (9) nine letter word they both pack much power. It is very clear in the Bible that it is, an act that God hates. Proverbs 6:16-19. But before we get to the word of God let's look at the definition of both of these words. Deception - the act of deceiving someone, a thing that deceives an act or statement which misleads. It hinders the truth. To be real with you it is often done for personal gain. Deceit- the action or practice of deceiving someone by concealing or misrepresenting the truth. Now understand this, two (2) words with the same definition. People deceive other people out of greed, hatred, jealousy, envy, and misunderstanding whatever the case may be its wrong.

Proverbs 6:16-19 NIV

16 There are six things the LORD hates: seven haughty eyes, a lying tongue, hands that shed innocent blood, 18 a heart that devises wicked schemes, feet that are quick to rush into evil, 19 false witness who pours out lies and a person who stirs up conflict in the community.

Gerald is a hardworking man, a man of great value and a man of honor and respect. One day as he was working around the house a young man came along and asks for his help. Gerald stopped what he was doing and helped the young man out. He helped the young man find a job, worked on his wife's car, but still this was not enough for the young man we will call Tracy. Tracy still wanted more. Gerald said to Tracy what else can I do for you? Tracy answers him, "man you make a lot of money." Gerald said I work every day to have what I want. Gerald told him when you get my age as long as you keep working you too can have things like this. Well, Tracy didn't want to work his whole life or to work his way to the top, to have what Gerald have.

Tracy is home and him and his wife, Linda, are talking at the dinner table about Gerald. Tracy says, "honey what do you think about this Gerald fella?"

Linda answers her husband, "I think he is a fine man, honey why you ask? He works every day, has nice cars and a decent house. Honey, we should be thankful to live around someone who cares. He's a great neighbor. Now on the other hand, the Whiteworths are another story, they are loud, no respect at all. Just because they have money, they think they can look down on everyone that lives near them, snobs s. I think Gerald is a plus to us."

"Linda, I think so too baby just wanted to see what you thought of him. You know honey I hear he has a lot of money, and we need to try to learn on how we can do the same. We need to get our share of the money too. I'm tired of working these five and dime jobs. Baby, you work too, and we barely make ends meet. We need to get our share now."

"Tracy, well baby what do you think we need to do?"

"Nothing right now baby I'm going to get to know Mr. Gerald a little bit better and see what's up with him."

Ok baby his wife says. Not knowing that Tracy was jealous and had greed in his heart towards Gerald. Tracy and her husband get in the shower together, but Tracy couldn't keep his mind off Gerald. He says, "honey this man is loaded. I want to be just like him."

Linda says, "come on, baby we in the shower. Can we keep Mr. Gerald out of our shower?"

"Ok baby, ok."

After they got out of the shower Tracy goes to the window to see if anyone is over Gerald's house, but no one was there. Tracy could not sleep at all that night he had things running in his mind. Working hard was not how he planned on making his living. He wanted to make his living off of someone else. "Tracy good night, honey and you need to come to bed and get out that window with your naked but, someone may see you." Tracy jumps in the bed; he couldn't sleep. He was too busy trying to figure out a way to get as much money as Gerald.

The next morning, they got up. "Tracy, good morning honey can you go down stair and make some coffee."

"You up already you go make the coffee."

"I like when you make it you make it better than me."

"Well since you put it that way, I guess I can drag my way out of bed to make my baby some coffee."

While Tracy is in the kitchen putting the coffee in the coffee pot, Linda yells downstairs for him to put some toast in the toaster so she can have some toast and strawberry jelly with her coffee.

Tracy looking out the window at Gerald's house sees he is already gone.

Tracy yells upstairs "Linda, are you coming back upstairs to get dress for work?" "Tracy yes baby, just taking the toast out of the toaster."

Tracy goes back upstairs to get dress he goes into the bathroom to brush his teeth. "Linda honey I love you and I want to make our lives easier. You work too hard at the hospital as a nurse. They don't appreciate you there. You come home every night tell me how hard you work, and you get no respect or honor from anyone, you come home sometimes drained and I'm tired of that, we haven't made love for 3 months baby, you always talking about you sooo tired. I'm tried to but when I want my wife, I need her."

"Tracy baby this will pass I'm working overtime so we can have enough money to keep our bills afloat."

Tracy finishes brushing his teeth and washing his face; he looks at the time and says, "Baby come on, I'm going to be late for my 10th day at work. I can't be late for 90 days; if so, I'm fired again, which can't happen!"

Linda grabs a cup of coffee and a slice of toast, puts some jelly on it and runs out the door behind Tracy. They are in the car.

Tracy says, "I wonder what time Gerald goes to work."

"Why have you become so interested in Mr. Gerald?"

Tracy says, "Oh, nothing, baby, nothing."

He drops his wife off at the hospital, kisses her goodbye, and heads for work. Tracy gets to work two minutes before it's time for him to punch the clock. Two men were in front of him waiting as well to punch the clock. Tracy yells and tells the men to move because he can't be late. One man moves, but the other man, Don says to him, na bro, you got to wait in line like everyone else and no favorers around here. Tracy gets mad, but he holds it all in because he knows he needs this job. His wife has been holding things down when he has been out of work.

Tracy tells Don, "Ok, Man, no problem."

Don says, "I know it's not."

Tracy gets upset and walks away, forgetting to punch in. At about 11:00 am, Tracy remembers that he didn't punch in, he tells his supervisor, and he tells him he will write it in for him. But his supervisor forgets, and at the end of the day.

The head supervisor comes to Tracy and says, "I see you on the job, but I don't see where you have punched in or written your time in." Tracy tries to explain to him that his supervisor told him he was going to write his time in.

"Well, well," the head supervisor says, "you don't know yet. You got to do things for yourself around here. Nobody is going to make sure your time is in. As long as their families get fed, they don't care about your family or your job."

Tracy says, "ok, man, ok."

The head supervisor replies, "I'm going to let you slide this time, but the next time I'm going to write you up."

"Ok, thanks, man, thanks."

Tracy writes his time in and leaves the job. He's on his way to pick up his wife from work, but his phone rings. It's his wife.

"Baby, I'll be working late again Ms. Corona called out sick; she is always calling out, and they need to get rid of her. She is 85 years old. She needs to be at home rocking on the front porch."

"Baby, ok, what time are you getting off?"

"11:00 pm."

Tracy says, "So I guess that means you will be tired tonight?"

"Baby, we need the money."

"You wait until this plan I have works. You are not working anymore for no hospital or anywhere else."

Tracy goes home he stops at the store to pick up some beer. He pulls up at his house and sees Gerald outside working on the front of his house, he asks Gerald if he need some help. He says, "Yea, why not you seem like a good neighbor." So, Tracy offers Gerald a beer and Gerald says, "Yes, you talking my language now." Gerald drinks the beer then asks Tracy if he has another one. Tracy sees Gerald is a drinker.

"Anytime you need someone to drink with or just to hang out with just let me know."

"Cool," Gerald says. Tracy goes home. Gerald goes inside to rest up before work. Gerald talking to himself, "Tracy may be alright to hang out with."

It's about 8:00 pm. Tracy lays down to get a nap before picking up Tracy. He wakes up, and it's 10:55 pm. No, no, I'm late picking up Linda. She is going to kill me. He gets in the car and calls Linda but no answer; he tries to call her again, but no answer. It is 11:00 pm. Tracy is not at Linda's job, so she picks up her phone to call Tracy, but she sees Tracy has been trying to call her.

Linda calls Tracy and says, "Where are you, Tracy? You know I get off work at 11:00. You should have been here waiting on me."

"Baby, you would not believe what happened. Gerald and I had a few beers, and I fell asleep, baby. I'm sorry. Please forgive me. It won't happen again."

"Ok, how long will you be?"

"I'm 15 minutes out, baby. I'm coming. I'm coming. Linda, ok?"

Linda goes downstairs to wait on Tracy, and a cop walks up to her. Cop's name is Pete. Pete says, "Hello beautiful, what is someone like you doing sitting outside? Linda tells Pete she is waiting on her husband to pick her up from work.

"I don't see a ring on your finger, Linda."

"I gained a little weight over the years, so I had to take it off."

"What kind of man can't buy his wife a new wedding ring?"

"We all gang some weight over the years."

"Honey, you are fine as wine with a little honey in it."

"Mr. Cop, I'm married and happy. Things happen that sometime people can't always be on time. GOOD, Sir."

Pete walks off. "If you need me, my number is 333-3131. Call me anytime, and I'll come get you in a dime." She shakes her head. Tracy pulls up. She gets in the car. Linda kisses Tracy. They drive home.

Tracy looks at Linda and says, "Gerald is not home; it's 12:00 am; where could he be this time of night?" What Tracy didn't know was that Gerald worked two jobs, so he wouldn't be home every night. "I'm going to find out a little more about Gerald."

"Baby, what has you so interested in this man?" Linda says.

"I don't know," says Tracy.

"I think you need to get Gerald off your mind and come inside so we can get ready for bed. You know you can't be late for work. You need to keep that job. We just bought this new house, and I can't pay for it by myself." Tracy goes in the house, still thinking about this man Gerald. As they enter the house, Linda says, "I'm going to take a shower to get all this work dust off of me."

"Can I get in the shower too?"

Linda says, "Yes, baby, come on." They get in the shower.

Tracy says, "oh baby, this shower is too hot turn some cold water on."

Linda says, "if you can't stand the heat, get out of the kitchen," and she laughs.

"I don't think that's funny."

"Baby, you know I like my water hot, then wash my back so I can get out, and you can turn the water down."

He starts washing Linda's back, then he moves a little closer to her, but Linda stops him and tells him she is tired, so she gets a towel and steps out of the Shower, leaving Tracy in the shower looking frustrated. Tracy finishes washing and gets his towel and gets in the bed. He tries to touch her in bed, but Linda tells him to stop.

"Linda baby, you say you love me, you want to be with me, then why I can't touch you?"

Linda says, "I just worked a 16-hour shift. My feet hurt, my back hurt, and my head hurt. Would you feel like someone jumping up and down on you?"

Tracy gets mad and jumps up out the bed naked and says, "when I get my money right, you going to be a stay-at-home wife, you hear me, Linda?" She says to Tracy I wonder when that will be! Tracy gets madder when Linda says that. So, he puts on his clothes, opens the front door and goes sit outside. Linda calls for Tracy to come back to bed, but Tracy doesn't hear her, so Linda falls off to sleep. Tracy is still sitting outside at two in the morning, wondering when Gerald is coming back home. He sees no lights on in the houses in the neighborhood, so he decides to go take a look around

Gerald's house. *The enemy is out prowling around, seeking to see who he can devour. 1 Peter 5:8.* But low and behold, there is that 85-year-old woman Ms. Corona that works at the hospital with Linda, only living two houses down from Gerald, sees Tracy going over to Gerald's house. She watches him run over to the back; it's too dark out, so she moves to another window, trying not to let him see her. Before He runs back to his house, he looks around to see if anyone is watching him; then he takes off running back to his house and locks the door. Linda never wakes up.

Ms. Corona thinks to herself why Linda's husband is over to Gerald's house this time of the morning. She wonders should she tell his wife or go to Tracy and tell him she saw him a Gerald's house the wee hours in the morning, or she thought I'll just tell Gerald. Well she didn't want to be seen like a trouble maker, so she decided to keep it to herself. She gets into bed. Still thinking about what she saw she could not sleep. Still wondering why Tracy was over to Gerald's house that time of night and Gerald not there. She slowly drifts off to sleep at 5:35 am.

It's 6 am. Linda gets up, goes to take a quick wash up and puts on her clothing and goes downstairs to make some coffee. Tracy is still asleep, she yells upstairs and tells him to get up, but he doesn't say anything. She gives him 5 minutes, but he still doesn't get up, so she runs upstairs to wake him.

"Come on, Tracy, we are going to be late for work. You are acting like you been up all night, come on get up," she says. Tracy drags himself out of bed, goes brush his teeth and washes his face. He looks at the clock and says, "Man, it's 6:45. Why you didn't wake me up when you got up, Linda?" Linda tells him, "I called for you to get up, but you never moved." Tracy is mad at Linda and says to her, "Can't get no nookie from my wife. I'm going to be late for work

11

on the 11th day. Boy, things are looking great." He never tells his wife he went looking around Gerald's house last night. They walk out the door, lock the door, and leave for work. Tracy drops Linda off for work, and he goes to work. He gets there 10 minutes late. He slips in with nobody seeing him. His supervisor comes. Man, we got work to do. We got to weld the side of this tank and have it ready by three before we leave for home. Tracy, man, there is no way we going to have this tank done by three no way. It's too big. The supervisor tells him if he stops running his mouth, we can get it done. Tracy wants to know what the other fellas are doing and why they are not here to help. The supervisor tells him it's not his duty to worry about what other employees are doing. He needs to worry about what he tells him to do. Now let's get it done. Tracy is mad but still working is about 3 o'clock now. Tracy didn't take a lunch break, and he knows that Linda gets off at four. He is not going to make it to pick her up on time, so he calls her and asks if she can stay a little longer today because he won't be able to pick her up at 4. Linda tells him, "Yes, baby, I can stay a little later. What time do you think you will be here?"

"About 5:30."

"Ok, baby, that's fine. Ms. Corona will be here. I can hang around with her."

It's five o'clock. Ms. Corona walks in the door, punches the time clock and goes to her desk. Linda smiles at her and says, "Hello, Ms. Corona. How are you today?" Ms. Corona looks at Linda strangely and says, "Hello, how are you and your husband?"

"We are well. We just moved into our new house."

"Really," Ms. Corona says.

"Yes, it's in a lovely neighborhood."

12

"That's great," Ms. Corona says. She didn't mention knowing about they live in the same neighborhood now or how she saw her husband running over to Gerald's house early that morning.

Linda's cell rings: she looks at it and sees it's her husband. She answers,

"Yes, baby?"

Tracy says, "I'm outside; come on."

"Ok, bae. My husband is outside. I hope you have a great day at work. See you tomorrow," Linda says.

Ms. Corona doesn't say anything just looks at her strangely. Linda walks out the door and gets in the car; she asks her husband how his day was.

He replies, "Hard work, hard work."

"Come on, baby; you got to work and stay on this job. We just bought our first house; I love it and want to keep it."

"Baby, I'm going to work things out to where you work when you want to work. You'll see." They pull up at home at about 6:30 pm and see Gerald outside working on someone's car, but no one is with him, so Tracy tells his wife to go in the house. "I'm going to talk with Gerald." His wife looks at him and asks, "why you keep going to his house? You don't know if he wants to be bothered."

Tracy says, "he told me we can have a few beers together. I'm going to see if he wants to drink with me. I can't get a nookie from you. I might as well get drunk. It'll take my mind off you and the damn job." Linda looks surprised, then asks him, "Baby, why you got to talk to me like that?"

"Oh, baby, I'm sorry; it won't happen again," Tracy says.

"Well, since you are going over to the neighbor's house, I'm going too."

"No, you go home."

"Why have I got to go home?" Linda says, "If you can go over to his house, I can too. It's not like I'm going by myself, you with me. So, let's go. I want to see what men talk about after a hard day of work."

So, they walk over to Gerald's house, and he looks up from under the hood of the car, wiping his hands and says, "What's up? What brings y'all to my house?"

Tracy says, "We just saw you outside and wanted to know if you wanted to have a couple of beers." Gerald tells him, "No, I don't drink when men bring their wives around just out of respect for the lady." Boy Linda's eyes opened wide; she says, "Such a gentleman," Boy Tracy did not like that. So, he says, "Well, we're going to go on across the street then." Gerald smiles at Linda and says, "Maybe next time when your wife is not with you." They walk back across the street. As they walk back, Tracy is furious with his wife. "I told you to go to the house. You just don't listen to anything I tell you. I saw how he looked and smiled at you. I saw you flirting with him on the sly." Linda gets mad and tells him, "You need to go take a ride and cool yourself off before you make me say something to you; you know, good and well, I only have eyes for you."

It's about 8:30 pm. Tracy gets in the car and rides out for a bit; he stops at a store and sees one of his old bodies who lived in the same neighborhood he did as a child. Tracy calls Randy, but he doesn't hear him. Tracy jumps in the car and pulls up beside Randy.

"Hey man, what have you been up to?"

"Tracy, is that you, boy? You sure gained weight over the year; what have you been up to, Tracy?"

"Nothing but working hard; got a new wife, a new job and new home things are looking good, man. What about you?"

Randy tells him he just got out of prison for armed robbery; "Man, I was down on my luck and couldn't find work, so I robbed a convenience store and got away with 15000.00 for 6 months until I went to the post office and someone so my picture on the wall and called the police. There I went to prison for 12 years. Man, it's hard out here when you have a felony, no job, no food, no shelter. I've been living here and there since I got out of prison."

"Man, let me talk to my wife and see what she says about you moving in with us until you get on your feet, I might be able to get you on where I work. They hire felons as long as you work."

"For the real man, you will do that for me."

"Oh yes, we go way back. We had some good times together; Tracy, here's my number. Call me in about two days. By then, I should have talked with her, and she should have had time to think it over."

"Ok, man, ok."

"You have some money;"

"Nope, man, not a dime in my pocket."

"Here, man, here's 90.00. Go get something to eat and a place to stay tonight. Now call me."

"I will, man, thanks."

Tracy drives off and heads back home. He gets home at about 10:45 and sees Linda is still up, looking over at Gerald's house and seeing he's gone slowly driving by and parking in his yard, backing his car in so he can see Gerald's house.

Linda looks out the window, sees Tracy, and calls him.

"Bay, why you are sitting in the car, at the house."

"Give me a minute."

"Ok, baby."

In the meantime, is about 11:30 pm now; Ms. Corona pulls into her driveway and sees Tracy sitting in his car; she's thinking, *why is he sitting in his car this time of night? Why is he not in bed with his wife?* She pulls into her garage, so he won't recognize her. The Bible tells us to be Matthew 10:16. "Behold I send you out as sheep in the midst of wolves. Therefore, be wise as serpents and harmless as doves." At about 12:00 am, she looks out her window with all the lights off in her house to see Tracy getting out of his car. She wonders why he keeps looking over at Gerald's house. *Should I call the police and tell them what's going on.* So, she sits there for a minute, picks up the phone, and calls the police.

"911 operator, this is Shirley speaking. What is your emergency?"

"My name is Ms. Corona. I live at 777 Bishop Drive," the operator says, "yes, ma'am. I can see. What's your emergency?"

"Well, I don't think it is an emergency, but I think it's a problem with my neighbor two houses down from me." Shirley says, "Is anyone hurt?"

"No," Ms. Corona says.

"Well, ma'am, you don't have an emergency; this line is only for emergencies." Ms. Corona hangs up. She gets into bed still wondering why Tracy is up.

It's 8:00 am. Ms. Corona gets out of bed, goes to the window, and sees Tracy and his wife have already left for work. She sees Gerald outside, sitting on his front porch, drinking something in a cup that looks like coffee. She puts on her clothes and goes out to meet him.

"Hi Gerald," she says.

Gerald says, "Hi, Ms. Corona, I don't see you out as much since your husband passed away."

"I don't get out as much anymore, just work and home pretty much." She wonders if she should tell Gerald that she saw Tracy around his house a couple nights ago.

"What's wrong, Ms. Corona? You look like you were in a daze a minute ago; is there something on your mind."

Ms. Corona replies, "oh no, nothing at all; I just wanted to stop over and say hello." "Have you met the new neighbors yet?"

"Oh yes, I work with his wife at the hospital and met her husband at a couple of Christmas parties."

"Oh, how cool is that great."

"Yes, I guess it is if you say so. They don't seem weird to you?"

"Oh no, from what I've seen, he and his wife seem to be ok to me. We had a couple of beers together, laughed, and went home. That house has been empty for so long I'm glad someone moved into it."

"Yes, I guess you're right, Gerald," Ms. Corona says, "Well, Gerald, I got to rest up for work this evening. See you later."

"Alright, Ms. Corona, see you later. She had not told Gerald anything about what she saw that night because she didn't want to

17

seem like a troublemaker in the neighborhood. She thinks to herself, *I'm going to watch Gerald's house. If I see anything going on suspiciously, I'm going over there with my gun and shoot their behind off. They better not mess with him. I'll go to jail over that man. He is a good man, and I'm not going to stand by and watch something happen to him all because the police say it's not an emergency. I'll blow Tracy off the face of this earth as God is my witness; I ain't playing now. I'll take matters into my own hands. I'm 85 years old. I've lived my life, my husband is gone, so I'm going to be the watcher of Gerald's house.*

On their way to work, Tracy tells Linda about Randy, but Linda doesn't like the idea, so she says let me think about it.

He says, "Come on, baby, he is a good friend of mine."

Linda says, "I didn't say no; I said, let me think about it."

Tracy asks, "How long you need to think about it."

"Come on, Tracy, give me a break. You just asked me 10 minutes ago. I'll tell you what. Give me till I get off work, and I'll let you know."

They pull up at Linda's job. She kisses Tracy goodbye and gets out of the car. Tracy is on his way to work when an unknown number comes up; he answers the call.

"Hello, Tracy, this is Randy; Man, you told me to call you."

"I just asked my wife about you this morning. Give me till tomorrow, and I'll call you to let you know what she says."

"Ok," Randy hangs up.

Tracy pulls up at work to see his supervisor outside, looking at the work he did yesterday. His supervisor tells him what a good job he did on that tank, "Man, you keep doing this. We may make you one of the supervisors around here." Tracy thinks, *I don't want to do this hard work all my life, but he smiles and goes to punch the clock.*

Mean, while at Linda's job, Pete, the police officer, has a gunshot victim that he brings in his police car to the hospital; Linda does not know it's Randy, the man Tracy had, asked to let come to stay with them. They rush him to the operating room, but he dies. The doctor asks Police Officer Pete what happen to him. He told him he was driving his normal route and saw him lying on the roadway.

"So, I put him in my car and rushed him over to the nearest hospital."

Linda asks, "What is his name?" Pete says all he could get out of him was Randy, but he had this number in his pocket and $20.00. Linda says, "This is my husband's number. What is he doing with his number?" She remembered that her husband had just asked if someone named Randy could come and stay with them. Linda says, "Let me go call my husband and tell him what has happened to his friend." She calls Tracy at work, but no answer.

"Well, I just wait and break the news to him when he gets off work."

"Mrs. Linda," Pete says, "can you please tell your husband to give us a call? We would like to know the last time he saw Randy alive."

"I'm sure my husband had nothing to do with his death; he just asked me this morning if he could stay with us until Randy gets back on his feet. I told him to let me think about it. Well, there is nothing for me to think about now. He's gone." She looks sad.

Back at Tracy's job, it's 3:30 pm. Everybody is running to the clock to punch out. Tracy gets there first; now, how's punching out first, he says to the two men who were at the clock the other day.

They just look at him and let him punch out then they all punch out behind him. He gets in the car and drives off. He gets to Linda's job, and she's sitting outside waiting on him. He hops out of the car, opens the door for her, and kisses her on the cheek with a big smile, "Hey honey," he says, "I had a great day at work." She says that's nice baby with a sad face. He asks her what's wrong she tells him she has some bad news.

"What is it?" Tracy asks.

"Well, you know your friend Randy the one you asked could he stay with us?" "Yes, baby, what?"

"A police officer brought him to the hospital today," Tracy asks before she can finish if he is alright. With her head down, Linda says, "No baby, he passed." "What? What? No, no, I was going to help him get a job, and he was going to help me out with something. Guess now I got to find someone else. Poor Randy, he was a good friend in school." They drive home.

"Baby, that's not all the police officer wants you to come into the police department and give a statement on when was the last time you seem Randy alive."

"Ok, baby, we'll go in the morning is Saturday, and we don't have to go to work." "Ok, baby."

They arrive home to see Gerald outside with some friends. They are playing cards and drinking, and the grill is smoking. Tracy asks his wife if he could hang out over Gerald's house for a minute. She says, "Yes, baby, after today, your friend passed away." He doesn't go in the house. He goes straight over to Gerald's house and asks him if it's ok to hang out there for a while. He tells Gerald about his friend dying today, and Gerald feels sorry for him and tells him to make himself at home "My house is your house." Tracy gets

20

a beer and sits down on the steps and watches them play cards. After a few minutes, someone asks him whether he knows how to play bid whisk. He tells them, "Yes, I'm a pro at any card games. But my favorite is spades." Gerald says, "One day, we can have you come over and play a couple of games with us. We play cards all the time when I'm not working." Tracy says, "Cool, I'll be here." Tracy gets another beer and another beer until he passes out. Gerald takes him across the street to his home. His wife opens the door and thanks Gerald for seeing him home. At about 10:30 pm, Linda puts him in bed and starts praying. "Lord, you know I haven't prayed in a long time, and I really need you to find out who killed Randy Tracy's friend. Protect us, Lord, because I feel something is just not right, amen." She gets in bed.

Saturday morning comes Tracy gets up with a headache he asks Linda how he got home she tells him Mr. Gerald brought you home.

"Man, I got to go and apologize to him, my second night over his house and I Passes out."

"Baby he was ok with that he was glad to see you enjoy yourself."
"Let's get dressed and get down to the police station so we can get this over with."

"Ok, I'm getting dressed now," she says.

Tracy runs and takes a quick shower he smells like beer from the night before. Linda goes down stair and makes a pot of coffee, she yells upstairs to asks Tracy if he wants a cup, he tells her yes.

"Come on baby I don't want to spend my whole day at the police station come on."

"Tracy I'm coming putting on my shoes now."

21

He falls down the steps on the way down and bumps his head to the rail. Linda screams. Gerald is outside washing his car and runs over to their house, bangs on the door and asks is everything ok. She says, "No, my husband just fell down the steps. Can you help me get him up?" But before Gerald could reach him Tracy hops up and tells them he is alright. Gerald says, "Man that is a nasty cut you should go get it checked out." Tracy tells them he's ok. "Well, if y'all need me later on just knock on my door I'm off today." They leave for the police station. Gerald goes back to washing his car. On the ride to the police station Tracy says so Gerald is off on Saturdays I see. Linda says look like it. They reach the police station Officer Pete is outside looking in his police cruiser. Linda introduces Tracy to Officer Pete before they go inside. "Come sit at my desk let me get a pad and pen so I can take your statement Sir." Officer Pete returns back to the table with a pad. "Ok. Sir," Pete says. "Let's get started. When was the last time you saw Randy alive?" Pete asks. "On the night of June 10th about 9:00 pm I stopped at a corner store and saw him walking and pulled up beside him and asks him how he was doing, he told me he had just got out of jail for armed robbery, and he spent 12 years in jail, I gave him 90.00 for some food and a hotel room. Man, I was going to see if he could move in with me and my wife."

"That's right officer he asks me that the same night he saw Randy and, on our way, to work yesterday morning. I told him I would give him and answer when I got off work yesterday," Linda looking sad, "but yesterday never came for Randy; he's gone."

"Officer did anyone see you talking to Randy that night?"

"I don't know it was dark and you know how these streets are at night. If you not in the city part of town you get no lights."

"Well, how did you get that cut on your head, I fell down the steps this morning," Tracy says.

"Really?" The officer says while shaking his head. "Ok,"I'll check around to see if anyone saw you that night. Don't try to leave town, we may need to bring you in for more questioning."

Tracy says, "Where I'm going? My whole life is here."

They leave and head back home. Tracy is worried.

"Linda, I hope he don't try to put this on me. I just feel funny about this."

"I feel the same way," Linda tells Tracy. "And you know what Tracy? I prayed for the first time in a long-time last night."

They get to the house and see Ms. Corona talking to Gerald. They get out the car and wave at them, Gerald yells and tell them to come over for a minute, Ms. Corona looks at Tracy crazy because she knows he had gone to Gerald's house and Gerald was not home. Gerald says,

"Ms. Corona was telling me that one of the police officers found a wounded person on the roadside."

"Yes, but they want release who it is because they have not found the next of kin." Linda and Tracy look at each other.

"We know nothing about that," Tracy says. "We have some unpacking to do so we have to leave know." Ms. Corona never opens her mouth; she just stands there looking crazy.

Gerald says, "Tomorrow we going to put something on the grill if you like to come by you can."

Linda says, "We will think about it." They go in the house leaving Gerald and Ms. Corona talking. Ms. Corona says, "Did you see their eyes when you say something about a person hurt? Man, I bet they had something to do with it, He looks like a killer anyway."

"No, No. Ms. Corona I don't think they even know anything about it. They seem to be good peoples to me."

"Well honey it's getting late in the evening, so I guess I better be getting in want to be in before dark."

"Ok, Ms. Corona be safe," he says.

"No, you better be safe you the one got people running around your house." "What you say?"

"O' nothing. I'm just playing." She speaks. They both say good night at the same time.

Back at the police station Pete is talking to another cop and tells him he found a man on the street wounded but by the time they got him into the operating room he dies. The other cop says, "Why didn't you call the Ambulance?"

"Man, I thought it would take too long for them to get there so I put him in my car and drove him to the nearest hospital."

"Man, that's crazy you know we were taught to never put anyone in our cars that is wounded unless we have a witness, they can say you killed him your word against theirs you know what I mean."

"I have a suspect who I think it is."

"Oh, really remember who you talking to. I know how dirty you are. Remember I used to be your partner."

Pete laughs and says, "No man I'm not that same cop anymore."

"Ok, man don't try to convince me it's you the one got to live with the guilt."

Pete says, "Ok, man I got to go." He Leaves and goes on patrol.

Linda and Tracy are at the home. Linda wants to go over to her girlfriend's house, so she asks Tracy if it was ok to take the car.

Tracy says "Sure, baby go head; I'm going to stay home and rest. May walk over to Gerald's house later on."

"Ok, honey see you later."

Linda says as she walks out the door. She gets in the car pulls out the driveway and head over to her girlfriend's house.

Proverbs 12:22 *lying lips are abomination to the Lord: but they that deal truly are his delight.* She's on the street of Deceitful Lane at the light. She sees the officer, Pete. He looks her way and yells, "Hey beautiful you left your hubby at home?" She ignores him and once the light turns green, she pulls off. Pete gets in behind her and follows her, but she doesn't stop by her friend's house because she doesn't want him to know where she's going. She calls her husband, but he is sound asleep. So, she heads back towards the police station, and he turns off. She parks her car and looks around then goes inside to tell the office at the front desk that an officer named Pete is following her. The officer laughs and tells her she shouldn't have been messing around with him he's one crazy cop. She tries to explain that she is married, and she has never had anything to do with him. The officer tells her to go home to your husband and leave Pete alone. She turns around and walks to the door and looks out to make sure she doesn't see Pete anywhere. She pushes the door open and runs to her car. She turns on the ignition. Pete runs up to her car and licks on the window. She pulls off as fast as she can and almost hits another car. Pete goes inside and the cop tells him to leave that woman alone because his job is at stake.

25

"Man, I'm just having a little fun."

"I think you playing with fire this time."

"I'll be alright I'm not going to do anything." The office asks him about the man that passed and if anyone found out who killed him.

Pete says, "No, but I have an idea."

The officer says, "Who?"

"The lady just left here. Her husband."

"Really man."

"Yes, really Pete says.

"Pete man you tell a lie so good I don't know if you are telling the truth or not." The officer says. "You'll see"

Pete says. "Well, our shift is over time to go home."

"Let's ride." Pete says. They both punch out and go home.

Linda makes it back to the house and her husband is still asleep, she rushes to the door and push the door open.

"Tracy, Tracy!" she runs upstairs, and Tracy jumps up out of bed.

"What's wrong, baby!? what's wrong!?"

"That cop that cop" Linda says, "that one that trying to say you killed Randy, he is after me."

"Baby stop playing."

"I'm not playing. He saw me at the light at deceitful Lane and was yelling all these crazy things to me then he followed me, but I never stopped by my girlfriend's house because I was too afraid to

26

let him know where I was going. So, I turned around and went to the police station and the cop there thought I was messing around with him and told me to go home to my husband. Baby, I'm scared."

Tracy grabs his wife and hugs her telling her it's going to be alright.

"Tracy, we have to do something!"

"Yes, baby we do if the cops want do anything about their crooked cop we will." "Come, I'll make you some warm milk so you can rest tonight. Would you like a little bit of cinnamon in it baby?" Tracy asks.

"Yes, please thank you."

"Go on upstairs I'll come up in a few to run you tub of warm water for a bubble bath."

She goes up stairs, sits on the bed, and starts to pray: *God if your real please do something about this Cop Pete, I don't know what I did to deserve this but God, I know you can fix it. Lord, I remember my grandmother praying to you night and day and she says you never let her down, so Lord if you're real don't let me down. Fight this battle for my husband and me.* Tracy brings the warm milk upstairs to his wife.

"What you doing honey?" Tracy asks.

"Oh, baby I was just praying to God hoping he hears me."

"Well baby I don't know about God, but I have a plan to where we can just leave this place and start FRESH."

Linda says, "How baby? We just bought a new house you just started a new job how we going to up and leave."

"You'll see I have a plain." Linda drinks her milk they both lay down holding each other. Tracy tells Linda it's going to be ok. It's about 10:30 pm. Linda drifts off to sleep. Tracy gets up and looks out the window to see if a light is on in Gerald's house, and it is. He puts on his house coat and walks downstairs. He calls Gerald, and he's still up. Tracy asks him can he come over for a few. "I have something I need to talk to you about." Ms. Corona Is looking out the window and she sees Tracy go over to Gerald's house, so she gets her a chair and sits in the window in the dark so no one will see her. She waits and wait but Tracy never comes out. She falls asleep sitting at the window. Tracy and Gerald are in the house talking and laughing, then all of a sudden Tracy asks Gerald how he got RICH. Gerald replies with two words: hard work.

Tracy says, "I ain't got time for *hard work*. I got to leave town for a few days and need some cash."

Gerald says, "How much cash you need?"

"About 800.00 to get me started" Tracy says, Tracy wanted to see what Gerald would say or he was trying to find out if he had any money in the house.

Gerald asks, "When you need it?"

"Now if you have it." Tracy says, "Me and my wife need to get away for a while." "Ok Cool man I got you," Gerald says.

Gerald goes to his room, closes the door and moves a board from the floor in the floor. There is a safe with about $75,000.00 in it. While Gerald is in the room, Tracy picks up a Rolex watch and puts it in his pocket. Gerald takes out $1,000.00 and puts it into an envelope. He gives the money to Tracy and says, "Here man, I hope this will help you out."

Tracy says, "Man, you must be loaded!"

28

Gerald says, "Nope, I just keep a little bit of money here just in case of an emergency."

"Oh' I see," says Tracy as he starts pacing the floor back and forth. Gerald asks him what's wrong, and Tracy replies nothing. They walk to the door with Tracy in front. Tracy is thinking that if he leaves the house now, he won't get another chance to get the money he came for. So, Tracy asks him about his job and if he can get him on. As Gerald is turning around, Tracy quickly grabs a metal lamp that is standing at the front door and hits Gerald over the head. They struggle. Blood is running down Gerald's face, Gerald faints. Tracy ties him up in the basement. Tracy goes back upstairs and heads straight to Gerald's room looking for the rest of the money, but he doesn't find it. So, he runs back downstairs to get the money Gerald put in the envelope. He looks out the window and doesn't see anyone then he runs to his house, not knowing the envelope has blood all over it. He takes the money out of the envelope, puts it in his pocket and stuffs the envelope in the bottom of the trashcan. Linda, still asleep, is unaware of what had just happened. He puts his pajamas on and gets in the bed like nothing has happen.

Ms. Corona finally wakes up. It's 3:30 am. She looks out her window and sees Gerald's light is still on. She sees no movement in the house, but she is afraid to go over because it is still dark outside. So, she keeps an eye on Gerald's house all morning. She goes to make her a cup of tea and goes back to her bedroom window waiting to see some movement; still nothing. She thinks to herself *what should I do? What if they're still in there getting drunk and I call the cops or what if I don't call the cops and something has happened? Its 4:30 am. I have about one hour before daybreak then I'm going over to Gerald's house just to make sure he's ok. Wait? Why did a light just come on at Tracy house? I'm going to set right here and watch. Boy, if they did something to my buddy, they're going to have to answer to me.* She pulls out her S &W 9mm out of the closet and sits it on her nightstand. *I mean that.* She gets mad, then she goes back to the window. She still sees the light on at Tracy's house.

Tracy wakes up Linda and tells her come on.

"Baby, we going to go on a little vacation and we not going to tell no one where we going."

Linda says, "what about our jobs?"

"Oh, baby you have leave. Just tell them you will be gone for about two weeks." "Baby I don't know if I can take off two weeks that's a long time."

"You still get paid, don't you?"

"Yes, but that is a long time for me to be away from my job people depend on me."

Tracy says, "well baby I too depend on you now."

She sits down and thinks for a while "Ok, I'll do it. I need a break anyway."

They pack their bags and walk out the door locking it behind them. They start the car and drive down the street. Ms. Corona gets her glasses so she can write down the tag number. She writes down a description of the car and their tag number as she reads it out loud. "Fl-3214. Blue. Ford. Edge. Got it!" *Come on day light I got to get to Gerald, now is 5:00 I can't wait any longer.* She puts on a small jacket, grabs her cell phone and walks as fast as she can to Gerald's house. She walks up the steps to find that the door is cracked open. She walks in slowly. "Gerald. Gerald... Gerald?" She walks in a little farther and sees blood on the steps, calling Gerald again but still no answer, she follows the trail of blood that leads to the basement. She calls Gerald again but still no answer. She walks to the other side and see Gerald lying on the floor with blood all over him. She quickly calls 911. Operator Shirley picks up again, "This is 911 operator Shirley. How can I help you?"

"This is Ms. Corona. There is something wrong with my neighbor! It's blood all over him!"

"Ma'am, what the address?" Shirley says.

"801 Bishop Lane, Anointed County."

"Ok, ma'am. I'll get someone right to you. Stay on the phone with me. Is he breathing Ma'am"? Shirley asks.

"I don't know! I don't know!"

Shirley tells her to calm down someone is on the way. "Can you see if he's breathing? Go a little closer and just feel his pulse on his neck or wrist."

"I don't feel nothing!" She says, "come on what taking them so long?" She calls Gerald's name again but still he does not answer. *I hear the Sirens! I hear the Sirens!* She runs as fast as she can outside so they wouldn't pass the house. They stop in front of the house. One man gets out and runs into the house. The other man gets out and pulls the stretcher out the back. As he's pushing it, he trips and falls. He gets back up and goes to the steps, the other man runs and helps him bring in the stretcher. They put Gerald on the stretcher.

"He is breathing!"

"Thank God!" Ms. Corona says. She gets in the Ambulance with Gerald. They arrive at the same hospital that Linda and Ms. Corona work at. They rush him to the operating room; they sedate him and start surgery. Ms. Corona goes to the waiting room.

It's 7:00 am; he's still in surgery. The officer, Pete, walks in and asks her to tell him what happened. She tells him she saw Tracy over Gerald's house around 10:30 pm. "He went in and was over there until I fell asleep, I never saw him leave. I woke up at 3:30 am and went to the window. I saw the lights on at Gerald's house. I know he always turns his lights off at night. So, I just sat in my window waiting for something to happen. Then, around 4:30 am, I saw a light come on at Tracy's house. I saw him, and his wife, Linda, leave with bags in their hands. You want their license plate number? I got it. Officer Pete says, "yes" as he continues to write everything down, she just told him. "Alright ma'am if we need anything else we will call you. What's your number?"

"333-3125" she says.

Now, it's about 9:20 am. Gerald is still in surgery. Pete calls an APB (all-points bulletin) on the blue Ford Edge tag number FI-3214. Linda and Tracy are still driving, they are in Texas now to make it to New Mexico. They stop on the side of the road because Tracy has to pee. He jumps out of the car and runs near the woods, by the time he turns around a man pulls up and asks them if they are ok. He looks at the car and remembers hearing something about a Blue Ford Edge on the radio back in FI. He doesn't say anything, he gets back in his car and calls 911.

Ten miles from the Mexico line they get stopped. Linda says,

"What's going on baby why are the cops pulling us over?"

Tracy says, "baby I don't know." But he really does know, he just didn't want to upset Linda. The officer gets out his car, walks up to Tracy's car and says, "Sir driver license and registration please." Tracy looks in his wallet and gets the registration and driver's license out, and hands it to the cop. The officer takes them back to his car and runs them in his cp, goes back to the car and tells them to come with him. Tracy asks him why. "Well sir this vehicle fits a vehicle that the Law Enforcements are looking for in Florida, come on sir, y'all need to come with me." Linda starts to cry. "What's going on? I never did anything in my life." The officer tells Linda all he knows that this car is wanted back in Florida. Linda says, "Baby, do you think this is Pete trying to put that murder on you?"

"Baby that could be it. But why is he after me?"

Linda says, "Baby that cop has been after me. He's been harassing me. I'm afraid." The policeman returns. "Come with me to the station and someone will come pick y'all up from there." Linda asks if they will be staying the night at the jail and the cop says yes. She looks at her husband with a frown.

Gerald is out of surgery and doing well, but he can't talk. The doctor comes out looking for Ms. Corona; she is fast asleep.

"Ms. Corona?"

"Yes?" She says in a soft voice.

"Gerald is doing well, surgery went wonderful" she jumps up.

"Can I see him?"

"Yes, but he will be in and out of consciousness until the anesthesia wears off." "Ok doctor" she says and walks to his room.

When she sees him, she starts to cry, his head all wrapped up in bandages. She gets close to him and whispers to him who did this, expecting him to answer. After a few seconds of silence, she pulls a chair over to his bed and sits there holding his hand. After about an hour he wakes up and sees her sitting there asleep. He lets her sleep. He hurts to think but he can't stop asking why he'd do this to him. If he needed more money all he had to do was to ask, I would have given him anything he wanted. Ms. Corona wakes up and sees he's awake.

"Oh, Gerald you are awake why you didn't wake me?" She speaks.

"I know you needed your rest, so I just let you sleep," he says. "Boy, my head hurts, what did they do to me?" He asks.

Ms. Corona says, "They had to do surgery to stop the bleeding, but the doctor says you are doing well, and you should have a full recovery."

"That's great," Gerald says.

Pete hears that Tracy and Linda are in custody at a Texas police station. He volunteers to go pick them up. The captain tells him to leave in the morning, but he insists on going tonight. The captain agrees with him, and he fills up his cruiser, gets a cup of coffee and a donut and heads to Texas.

Pete has been driving for three hours. He gets sleepy and runs off the road twice. So, at the next gas station, he stops to get him a soda and a bag of chips, while there he fills the cruiser back up. And continue on driving. He arrives at the police station, gets his paperwork for the two and gives it to the clerk at the front desk. They release both of them into the custody of the cop. Linda asks about their car. Tracy still has not told Linda what he did. The cop says, "You won't need your car, we will send someone to pick it up." They all get in the police car, Tracy in the back and the cop makes Linda get up front. They've been driving for two hours, the cop pulls off on a deserted dirt road, makes Linda get out the car and pulls the gun on Tracy and says, "If you say anything, I'll kill her you understand?" Tracy looks at him with his hands cuffed behind him feeling helpless. *Only God knows what he is getting ready to do with my wife*, he thinks. The cop makes Linda get on the ground with the gun to her head. Tracy is watching and kicking the window and trying to find a way out of the cruiser but there is no handle on the inside of the vehicle, tears run down his eyes. The cop tells Linda to dance with the gun to her head, she starts dancing and crying begging not to be hurt. He licks her face while she dances then he tells her to go get back in the car. She runs back to the car. The cop laughing at Tracy says, "What kind of man leaves his wife waiting after she gets off work?" They say nothing else to him then pull off. They get back on the main highway and drive to an old store that looks abandoned but when they get inside it's not abandoned at all. "This is where I take all the people I want to kill after I finish with them", he tells Tracy and Linda. Tracy is still handcuffed, and ankles cuffed too. He is wondering what he can do to get him and his wife out of there. The cop's cell phone rings, it's the captain.

"Just checking on you everything ok?" He has the gun to Linda's head and gives the both of them a look, like if you say anything I'll blow her head off.

"Captain everything is ok, we're on our way there soon. We going to stop to get something to eat then we will be on our way," the captain asks if he thinks that is a good idea.

"Oh yes sir it is a wonderful idea everything is fine sir, its fine."

Once convinced the captain hangs up. The cop makes Linda go to the sofa and rapes her with Tracy watching. Tracy gets up and runs to his wife. The cop points the gun at him and tells him to stop or he'll shoot. Tracy stops in his tracks. Linda crying puts her blouse and pants back on. Tracy and Linda look at each other. Tracy is mouthing "I'm sorry."

"That's what a man gets that leaves his beautiful wife waiting on him."

They leave the place and get back in the car. Linda is still crying softly. Tracy feels helpless. Now the cop says, "I got something to tell you." He laughs," your friend Randy? I killed him and I am going to frame you. Tracy, you going down and I'm going to have you wife all to myself, Linda if you say something I will have you in jail with him and tell them you was accessory to the fact. So, you better be quiet when we get back to the jail. Oh' yes, Ms. Corona told me about you going over to Mr. Gerald house and she never saw you leave, you beat that man with his own lamp, didn't you? We have the lamp as evidence. You left him to die, you better hope he lives; if he doesn't you will be charged with two murders." The cop laughs, shaking his head. Linda is in disbelief, she screams, "Noooo! Tell me you didn't do that Tracy! Tell me you didn't do that Tracy!" Linda is crying and rubbing her head. Tracy never says a word to Linda. They keep driving and they make it back to the police station. "Linda if you don't want to see your husband die keep your mouth shut."

So, the next day it's time for Gerald to go home and Ms. Corona agrees to look after him while he recovers. She calls Uber to pick them up. The nurse comes in with his discharge papers, he sees them get him a wheelchair,

Gerald says, "I can walk."

The nurse says, "This is our procedure, we must do this for your safety and the safety of the hospital." She takes him to the front. Ms. Corona sees the Uber and flags her down. She pulls up to where they are standing and puts on her flasher. They get in the car. The Uber driver says,

"What happen to you?"

"Gerald won't say anything," Ms. Corona says, "Are you ever going to tell what happened to you? You don't have to tell me I know that Tracy guy tried to rob you."

The Uber driver says, "Tracy and Linda? They have an APB out on them."

Ms. Corona says, "I hope they find them!" Not knowing they were already in custody at the police station.

They get home and the Uber drive helps Ms. Corona get Gerald in the house.

The Uber driver says, "Oh my God what happened here."

Ms. Corona says, "He won't tell no one."

The Uber driver says, "I can stay to help you clean this up if you like."

Ms. Corona agrees to be helped "Thank you, because he can't clean right now, he needs to get some rest." Gerald goes up stairs to lie down. They start cleaning and scrubbing down the house. It takes 3 hours to clean the house, they get all the blood up, put everything back in place and wash the bloody lamp off. The Uber driver says, "If you don't need me for anything else, I'll be leaving, got to go make my money." She leaves. Ms. Corona goes to check on Gerald to make sure he's ok. She walks in the room to find him sound asleep. "I'm staying here with you tonight." She gets his key, locks the door and then walks down to her house to get some clothes.

They enter the police station: Linda, Tracy and then Pete. The cop at the desk asks, "What took you so long? That's only a 6-hour ride from here." The cop doesn't say anything. The officer behind the desk looks at Linda and she looks away because she doesn't want to get her husband killed. The cop Pete motions them to go over to the other desk. "I need to get some information from you." He sits at his desk, pulls out some paper and starts to ask Tracy questions about the Gerald case.

"Where were you on the night of June 11th?"

Tracy says, "Home with my wife, until 10:30 pm I went over to a buddy's house that lives in the neighborhood, why?" Tracy asks.

"There was an assault on your neighbor. Someone tried to kill him."

Who was this person?" Tracy asks.

"What?" Linda says, "is he ok?"

"I don't know." the cop says.

It wasn't me, says Tracy, when I left Gerald's house he was ok. Maybe a little drunk but ok.

"So, you're telling me you didn't do it?"

"Yes, that's what I'm saying."

Then he turns to Linda and starts asking her questions.

"Where were you the night of June 11th?"

"Home sleep" she says.

The phone rings and it's the tow man.

"Where do you want me to drop the car at?" Pete the cop tells him to leave it in front. "Now who going to pay the fee?" Pete gives Tracy the phone. The tow truck driver says, "Sir, your bill is $700.00. We towed your car 375 miles that's about $1.87 a mile sir, you can do the math." He tells Tracy he'll take off $1.25. Tracy repeats the total and glances at Linda. Linda interjects in a whisper, "we don't have that right now." Tracy tells her not to worry and pays over the phone. Tow truck driver tells him a receipt will be available during processing to leave. Linda looks at Tracy like *where you get that money from*, but she never says a word. Pete slightly disappointed says, "I can't book you on what an 85-year-old lady says, she may be touched in the head." Then he gets quieter, "If I find out that anything she says has some truth to it, Tracy, your wife will be mine and there is nothing you can do about it." The cop tells them they can go for now but if he hears of anything else they're dead. The other cop at the front desk was watching Pete take the information down and feels like something just doesn't seem right. As Tracy and his wife walk toward the door, Pete goes to the restroom, the other cop hands Tracy a note with instructions to call him.

Ms. Corona opens her door. She walks in the house and sees how she last left it. She prepares some coffee, Tea and biscuits then goes upstairs to pack a light bag. Before leaving she looks around to make sure she has everything she needs. "Wait a minute I forgot to get my piece!" She runs back upstairs to get her gun. "Won't nobody mess with him tonight." She walks out of the door, gets in the car and drives back to Gerald's house. She uses Gerald's keys and opens the door. She puts her things down and goes to check on Gerald, he's still resting. She goes into the kitchen to enjoy tea and biscuits she brought from her house then, she falls asleep. Thirty-five minutes into her nap She hears some noise outside, so she gets up to look out the window. It's Tracy and Linda getting out of the car. She watches them take their bags out the car, she runs to get her gun and returns to the window and says, "Come over here tonight, somebody is going to die, and it won't be Gerald or me." She doesn't go back to sit down until they go into the house.

Linda and Tracy get home they put their bags down and both sit in the great room, looking at each other. Linda asks,

"Tracy did you do anything to Ms. Gerald?"

"No, he was perfectly fine when I left."

"Baby you wouldn't lie to me would you."

Tracy says, "No, no I didn't touch that man. He's a good man. Why would I want to harm him?"

"Ok baby just making sure. I'm so sorry someone wants to harm him. Baby you think we chose the right neighborhood?"

Tracy hugs his wife and says, "Yes this is a great neighborhood, you don't have anything to worry about."

Linda asks Tracy, "What are we going to do about what happened to me? I feel nasty and dirty. I'm going to get in the shower."

"No baby you can't, yet. Let me call the cop first."

"But baby if we tell anybody he's going to kill you, but I know we got to do something."

"We can't let him get away with this, baby. This man raped and assaulted you. That is 20 to 30 years in prison." Tracy says.

"Do you really think they are going to do something to one of their own men? I think not." Linda says.

Tracy picks up the phone and calls the number, Detective Johnson answers.

"This is Tracy, you gave me your number as me and my wife was leaving the station tonight. something happened to me and my wife on our way back from New Mexico last night. Sir I don't know if I can trust you can I trust you sir?" Tracy asks.

The cop starts to list the offenses being held against Pete.

"You're one of many. He raped an 11-year-old girl, he killed three men, he stole $100,000.00 worth of property. He had two drug dealers killed because they wouldn't do what he wanted them to do. This cop is nothing to play with. I saw your wife come in a couple of days ago telling me that he was following her." Tracy says he knew Pete was trouble. Linda nods in agreement.

"So, Tracy what happened?"

"I was handcuffed and couldn't do anything. We get in the car, and he tells us that he killed my friend Randy and was going to put the crime on me. So, he could have my wife. Then as we drive a long, he pulls over on this dirt road and makes my wife get out the cruiser and holds a gun to her head and tells me if I say anything he will kill her. He makes her dance for him then he licks her on her face and tells her to get back in the car. We drive again to a remote place, and it looks like it is an abandoned building but is not. He has it set up like a hotel room." Tears start to roll down Linda and Tracy's face. "He raped her. I was handcuffed. There was nothing I could do. I no longer feel like a man."

"We need someone to testify against him. Will y'all do it?" He asks.

Tracy looks at Linda, Linda says "but he says he will kill you then he will have me all to himself I don't want that." The cop assures Linda that the only reason they can't get him, is because people won't testify.

"Ma'am that is the only way we can get him. He raped you terrorize your husband, kill your husband friend and was going to frame your husband for it that is enough to put him away for life or better yet lethal injection. This man doesn't need to be on the street

41

but unless we can get someone to testify, he will keep on doing it. The police department doesn't care the only time they care is when they find someone to testify."

More tears run down Linda's face she says, "yes I'll do it." The cop tells them to come back the station so they can go to the hospital.

"No!" Linda says, "He may find out and come back for us." The cop assures Linda that won't happen, and no one will find out, it is totally confidential, and that Pete won't know until court. Her husband gets up and walks towards her and hugs her. "It's going to be all right baby, we got to do this for all the people he has hurt and gotten away with it, just think how many people we will be saving from him, the monster cop." They sign the paperwork and finish giving their statement. "There will be an undercover cop driving a white Toyota supra. His name is Zim. If you need anything I mean anything. Just call out. He doesn't know your case, but he does know it's high profile. He's one of the best."

They leave the police station and go to the hospital. Linda pleads not to go to the hospital she works for. Detective Johnson assures her they we would never do that. "It's in a center many witness protection people use. No one knows about it. And you will have a hoodie on, no one will know. They get in the car and head for the center. It takes them 20 minutes to get to the center, it's dark out and you can't even see your hands. They push a button, and a lady answers.

"How can I help you?"

"Sharon this is Detective Johnson." She buzzes them in. They walk up a long green hallway into a calming pastel yellow room. The doctor comes out. She already knows Linda needs a Rape test done please. She asks Linda her name and sends her and her husband into the examining room.

"Can we explain What happened? the doctors says.

Tracy says, "We would rather not talk about it."

The doctor says, "Do you know how a rape test is completed?"

Linda shakes her head no. "Well, that's fine. I'll explain it as we go. Here is a robe I'll leave the room while you undress. I'll return when I think you are ready. Your husband can stay. You can talk about it with him." Tracy uses that as his cue.

"Linda, are you ok with going through this?" Tracy asks.

Linda pauses for a moment ---- then says, "Yes, I'm ready. He's going to pay for what he did to us and those other people." She undresses and gets on the table. Tracy calls for the doctor to come back in. The doctor begins her examination and opens the robe up. She sees the bruises on her. The room remains silent.

"Ok It's just like you go to your OBGYN doctor we are look for bruises on the inside wall, forced entry with scarring or torn tissue, semen for the other person and we going to take some pictures."

"Of my face?" Linda says.

"Oh no not of your face just your body where the bruises are." After several minutes the exam is over. "I have all I need, sealing it up and sending it to the lab now. You may get dressed." She gets dressed and they look at the time and it's 4:30 am. They walk out the examining room, Detective Johnson is waiting for them. Linda says, "I'm ready to go home." Detective Johnson says they can go. "I'll pull you right up beside your car when I get you back to the police station, so you won't have to walk." While driving along, Linda says,

43

"I can't wait till this is over."

"Everything is going to be alright," Tracy says. They get out of the cruisers and get into their car and go home. It is about 6 am.

Ms. Corona wakes up and looks at the clock. it's about 6:30 am. "Wow," she says, "I must have really been tired." She goes to check on Gerald. He's sitting up in bed.

"Good morning how are you feeling?" she says to him.

"Oh, my head hurts like crazy," he says. She tells him how he just had surgery. Gerald says, "All I need is a cup of coffee." She goes to the kitchen to make some coffee and she hears a car pull up. she runs to see who it is. It's Tracy and Linda, she says to herself. She runs outside and starts arguing with Tracy and Linda insisting Tracy tell the truth about what happened to Gerald.

"I know you did it!" She yells.

Tracy says, "I told you it wasn't me!" Ms. Corona squints, shows him her holster then goes back into Gerald's house to finish the coffee and prepare something for breakfast. She takes his food into the room and Gerald starts to eat.

"MuM this food is delicious," he says still stuffing his mouth.

"Gerald, can I ask you a question about that night?"

"What night the night the assault took place?"

"Yes," she says.

"Go ahead." Gerald says.

"What happened to you that night?"

He pauses. "I don't know," says Gerald, "I really don't know." He takes another bite of food. Gerald tells Ms. Corona to never speak of it again until it's over.

"Are you finished eating", Ms. Corona says.

Gerald replies "Yes, thank you so much, the food and coffee was really good, reminds me how my mamma would make them." Ms. Corona laughs goes into the kitchen to clean up while Gerald watches Superman Return from Kryptonite Valley.

The doctor calls Detective Johnson and tells him Linda's results are back.

"Great. put them in a safe place until we can get this thing sorted out. Ok?" Detective says.

"We have a safe here, it will be here when you need it." the doctor says.

"OK. Thanks so much this means so much to me."

The Detective calls Linda and tells her the results are in and they are in a safe place. His phone rings and it's the cop Pete.

"Hello, Detective Johnson," he says.

"Yea man this Pete I need to talk to you. I need you to help me build this case on that Tracy guy."

"Hey Pete. What do you need me to do?"

"Well, he was the last one who saw his friend Randy alive so I need him to be charged for this crime." Pete says.

"Why do you need him charged for this crime? Are you sure he, did it?" Detective asks.

"Yes, man I'm sure," Pete says aggressively.

"How are you sure? Did you see him at the crime site?"

"No, but I know he did it." Pete says confidently.

"Well, Pete you on your own. I've cleaned up enough of your messes. You got to take care of this one on your own."

"Wow, it's like that man?" Pete says.

"Yes, it's like that. When have you ever helped someone else out it's always about someone helping you out. Nah man I can't do it," says Detective Johnson.

Pete comes from out of nowhere, pushes him and grabs him by his throat. Detective Johnson breaks loose, and they scuffle. Two other officers come and break them up, but not before Johnson whips his butt. Pete laughing and wiping blood from his nose says, "Man I thought you were a punk you do have a little fire in you." Pete continues to laugh as he walks out the door. Detective Jonson says," That fool is crazy for putting his hands on me." He leaves to make his stop at Tracy and Linda's house.

Tracy and Linda are at home cleaning the house when a white Toyota supra pulls up. Zim gets out, knocks on the door and introduce himself,

"Hi, I am Zim with the special unit department, I will be outside somewhere in your neighborhood just in case you need me, you won't see me, but I can see you and your house when you get in the car if you outside in the yard. Just feel safe to come out, you don't have to be afraid."

"That makes me feel a lot better," Linda says. He gets back into his car and drives into a remote area and sets and watches the house. After about 20 minutes he sees Pete drive up and keep driving back and forth by their house. He calls Detective Johnson,

"Hey man what's going on with Pete he keeps driving by Tracy's and Linda's house."

"Man, that is a long story," Detective Johnson says. "He should not be over there at all, just stay and watch them to make sure he doesn't go inside.

"He's getting out and putting something in their driveway."

The Detective says, "after he leaves, please don't say anything to Tracy or Linda about what just happened, if they didn't see him just get it and we can use it in court against him."

"About time someone is ready to fight back. That family he paid off. Man, that was my little cousin's daughter. Man, that was messed up, especially when you don't have anything and you see no way out, and money comes along, they took $75,000.00 from Pete and settled the case out of court, crazy man crazy."

"Yea, I know but hopefully we have this case solid." Detective Johnson says.

Zim says, "He just pulled off Give me 2 minutes let me go see what he put in their yard." Driving down the street Pete sees Zim but he doesn't recognize him, so Pete keeps driving. He pulls up on the side of the road, picks up the brown bag and gets back in the car. He drives off and calls Detective Johnson back.

"Hey, man I got the bag." Zim looks in the bag. "It's a gun. We got him now."

"That may be the gun he shot Randy with. I'm on my way to their house. You go back up the street and I'll pick it up from you and take it to the lab to have it tested. Stay with them, until I get there, then you can go get something to eat and come back. I'm 10 minutes out," Johnson says.

Gerald gets up and walks in the kitchen where Ms. Corona is cleaning. She tells him to go back to bed, but he doesn't listen.

"I can't stay in bed too long." He pulls out a kitchen chair and sits down slowly, "and I got to do something" he says.

"Well, you're not going outside" she says. He doesn't disagree.

"Ok," he says," Well I need you to go do something for me."

"What is it?" she says.

"Go to Tracy's house and ask him to come over for a minute not sure he will but asks anyway. I really need to talk to him. Tell him I said everything is ok." She wants to protest, but she wants to know the truth too. So, she goes downstairs and opens the front door and walks across the street, knocks on the door, Linda comes to the door.

"Oh, Hi Ms. Corona, I hope you doing well. What can I do to help you?"

"Gerald wants to talk to your husband."

"Ok I'll go get him", she walks towards the back of the house,

"Honey Gerald wants to talk with you."

He walks to the door. "Do you know why he wants to talk with me."

"No, all I know is he asked me to come over and get you."

"Ok I'll walk over there and see what he wants." Hesitating as he slowly walks over to his house. Knocks on the door Gerald tells him to come in. Tracy looks around and sees that there's no blood or signs of a struggle anywhere. Linda and Ms. Corona talk outside and exchange laughs. Ms. Corona says,

"Do you know what happened to Gerald?"

"Yes, I heard about it. I wonder who would do such a thing?" Linda says.

"MuM," Ms. Corona says, "I KNOW WHAT I THINK BUT Gerald told me not to mention it again. So, I will leave it alone. That's my buddy and he has his reasons."

Gerald tells him to sit down. "Man, tell me why you do this to me. Thought we were going to be good neighbors." Tracy starts to explain to Gerald why he did it. "This cop killed my friend Randy and he's trying to frame me for it because he wants my wife," Tracy stars crying, "He raped her too!"

"What?" Gerald says.

"I feel so helpless because he's an officer and if I go after him, I'll be the one in jail. Man, all I wanted to do was to get enough money so Linda and I could leave town, I had plans on never coming back to this place. Man, I'm so sorry for what I did to you man I'm sorry. You have been a good neighbor to me. Look what I did to you." Tracy falls down on his knees praying to God asking for forgiveness. He gets up. Gerald looks at him. Tracy says,

"Man, I did this, and I have to pay for what I did to you. I'm sorry. If you want to call the cops now you can."

"No, this is what I'm going to do, I have some buddy on the force I'll talk with them and we are going to get this cop, by the way who is he, what's His name?" "Pete" Tracy says.

"Pete?" Gerald says, "that's the same guy who raped that little girl and got away with it."

"Now we gotta get him this got to stop."

"Wait one minute let me call Zim." He dials Zim's number. Zim answers and greets Gerald.

Hey, Zim. My neighbor Tracy is at my house and he's telling me some things about Pete. Tell me what's going on so I'll know he's telling me the truth."

Zim says "He's telling is the truth. I'm working with them now. I'm watching their house; Johnson is the one handling the case. Man don't say anything to him because we don't want them to know that Pete was already by their house, he left a gun in their yard in the bushes. I saw him do it. I called Detective Johnson, and he knows I went and picked up the gun. We have him now. Johnson is on his way to their house as we speak."

"Ok Zim just wanted to know." Gerald turns around and looks at Tracy. "This is what I'm going to do. I'm going to help you get out of this one. Only because I see you trying to make a life for you and your wife. Don't nobody have to know what happened here. We going to put all of this in God's hands and let him work it out. That's where it will say you understand. But from here on, you are not allowed in my house alone with me anymore because the next time is going to be you pushing up daisy. Don't take what I'm saying to you lightly. You won't get a next time. The only reason I'm doing this is because God gave me a second chance. Here is yours, live it the right way."

Detective Johnson pulls up. Zim pulls up behind him. He gets out of his car and quickly hands the bag with the gun in it to Detective Johnson while he is still sitting in his car. He puts it in his glove compartment and locks it. Zim leaves to go get lunch. Johnson gets out of the car and sees Ms. Corona and Linda talking. They both speak to him then Ms. Corona walks back to Gerald's house. She opens the door and yells upstairs. "Tracy some Detective is over your house!" Tracy looks out the window and sees it's Detective Johnson and shakes Gerald's hand and thanks him. He runs out of Gerald's house and across the street back home to meet the Detective.

"What's wrong man, is everything ok?"

Detective says "Yes everything is great, your test results are back. Linda has given us permission to discuss the results. The examination shows forced entry and with all the bruises we got him!"

Linda says, "Thank God I've been praying that they get him!"

Tracy says, "Thank God. Maybe we can live in peace."

Zim is on his way to get something to eat at Divine Cafe and sees Pete there. Pete recognizes the car from seeing it near Linda and Tracy's house, he waits to see who it is. It is Zim.

"Zim what are you doing on this street?" He asks. Zim tells him his wife's cousin lives on that street.

"What are their names?" he asks.

"Larry, why are you asking?" Zim says.

"Nothing. I just like the neighborhood and think about buying a house in that area." Pete says.

Zim says, "Nice area I can see who's making all the money, wish I could afford a house in that area."

Pete says, "You know how we do!"

Zim says, "No, I don't know how we do. Enlighten me!"

Pete says, "let me get my goldfish plate and take it back to the other side of town and eat." He leaves.

Zim gets his fish sandwich then returns to his car. He rides back to his spot where he can see Tracy and Linda's house then prepares to wait. Zim calls Detective Johnson to let him know he is back in the spot by Tracy's and Linda's house.

"Ok good I'm leaving their house now I'm going to the DA to get this ball rolling." Zim says "Great, can't wait to see him in ORANGE." Detective Johnson turns to Linda, "Remember if you need anything, Zim is just a second away. "Linda nods as she opens the door for him. He gets in his car and goes back to the office to talk to the DA.

Pete gets back to the police office and sits down at his desk to eat. One of the cops comes by and sees his plate and asks him where he got it from. Pete says, "My favorite spot in the hood, that's my side of time: I run that!" He says laughing.

"What's the name of it? I would like to go get a plate."

Pete says, "Divine Café."

The cop says, "You have the address."

Pete writes, "108 Earl Franklin Dive."

"Got it on my way there."

Detective Johnson pulls up at the station and sees Pete's car there. He gets out and walks into the station and sees Pete sitting there eating. Pete looks up at him and smiles and continues eating. Detective Johnson knocks on the DA door she says come in. The Detective tells her what's going on with the case and what Pete did. She asks him, "Do you have someone that will testify against him? I want him off the force. He gives us a bad name. People think all cops are bad, some yes but not all". She looks at Johnson and says, "Get the paperwork together let's take him down." Pete sees a Detective talking to the DA and gets up from his desk and walks in her office. Pete says, "What's going on in here? You been in here a long time Detective." Detective Johnson leaves the DA's office and starts building the file on Pete.

The DA gets upset with Pete because he didn't knock. She gets up out of her seat and tells him to go back out the door and knock, "You don't run anything around here, this is my office and if everyone else knocks you will too." He walks out of the office laughing. He goes back to his desk and finishes eating then goes home.

He thinks, *something is up because everyone round here is too quiet. Let me see if I can find out what's going on.* He walks in his house and gets right on the phone. He calls two of the officers who work different shifts. He asks them if they have heard anything going on around the office. They both tell him no. He's not satisfied with their answer, so he calls someone else. She tells him no it's been quite lately. She asks him why he asks. He says, "Its nothing." She hangs up the phone and looks at her husband.

Linda's brother Terrance and his friend Timothy comes over to visit. Tracy tells Linda not to say anything to her brother about what happened. Tracy opens the door and invites them in. "Hey guys come on in." They walk to the great room, where Linda is and sits down. Linda was very quiet, so Terrance asks her what's wrong. She says nothing, but he keeps asking her, so she breaks down and tells him. He jumps up and says,

"I'm taking care of this. It's going to be alright."

Linda says, "Please don't tell my husband please."

"Don't worry I got this."

Tracy walks in the room and sits down with some beer and some pork skins. They eat, drink and laugh. It's getting late and I'm going to be getting on now. They leave. Linda gets the beer cans up and takes them and puts them in the trash. Tracy walks up behind her and gives her a hug. He Tells her it is going to be alright. And now She knows it will. They go upstairs and get in the bed.

Terrance and Timothy while on their way home is thinking of a plan to get Pete. They come up with a perfect plan.

"We are going to set him up," says Timothy. "I have the perfect person", he says. Terrance asks who he has in mind. Timothy pulls out his phone and shows him a contact: Beloni.

"Are you sure you want to get her involved? You think she will do it?"

"Yes man we cool like that, I helped her out with something, and she owes me a favor." He calls her. She answers in the second ring.

"Hey baby girl we need you to help us out with something it's very important," "Boo you know I got you, you helped me out. What do you need me to do?"

"I just need you to get this cop to take you on a date and we will handle it from there."

"Who is this cop? What has he done?"

"A cop named Pete works at station 321. And I can't tell you that all you need to do is get him to take you on a date."

"Wait a minute is that the one who raped that 11-year-old little girl?" Terrance tells Beloni yes. She says, "oh yes I will, where what time and what place."

"He will be on duty at 7 am and he always go to Lashea's donut shop at 9 am."

"I'll be there in the morning."

Detective Johnson is turning all the paperwork into the DA, as she looks it over, she tells him that it looks like we got him this time. The DA calls Tracy and asks him if he and his wife are sure they want to go through with it. Tracy tells her, they're sure.

"After we found out what he did to that 11-year-old girl my wife and I are."

"Ok that's all I needed to hear."

"Detective, take one of the other cops with you and go see if he's on his beat. If he is there, bring him in for questioning. Please do everything right because we don't want him to get away this time. Read him his rights and bring him in. I want him bad," she says.

He takes another cop with him so he can drive the cruiser back to the station and just in case he has a problem out of him. They drive around looking for Pete but no Pete and no Cruiser. They drive around to all the places they think he would be but no Pete anywhere to be found.

Beloni gets to Lashea's Donut shop at 9:00 am the same time Pete gets there. She gets out of her car and walks inside. Pete gets out of his car and walks inside. In the meantime, Linda calls her brother and tells him, "I know where we can take him, the same place he raped me at. It is a remote place. No one will know we are there." Her brother says, "Are you sure you want to go?" "Yes," she says.

Pete walks up to the counter where Beloni is and calls her a beautiful lady. She thanks him. He says,

"What's your name?"

She says "Destiny."

"What a pretty name for a cinnamon bun I can just eat you up."

She says, "I'm free, maybe you can take me for a ride in your cruiser I would like that."

"You really want to go for a ride in my cruiser", Pete says.

"Yes, I just told you I was free. I love a cop who is not afraid to take chances. That's my kind of man", she says.

"You are speaking my language now. I love a woman who is not afraid to walk on the wild side. I'm going to show you something you have never seen before."

She laughs. "Is it ok if I ride with you?" He smiles and confirms with a nod and grin. "I'm going to get my coffee and run to the bathroom really quick,"

"Ok, I'll be waiting in the car," he says.

She enters the bathroom and pulls out her phone and calls Timothy,

"Hello, Timothy I got Pete. I'm going riding with him in his car. I need y'all to come pick my car from Lashea's donut shop."

"Ok we're on the way. Put the keys under the mat."

"Will do," she says. She walks out. "Pete is really waiting for his Destiny," she says, "give me one minute let me get my phone." She goes and puts her key under the mat. She walks to the car and looks around to see if anyone is watching her get in the car with him.

"I'm ready," she says.

"Let's go." Pete says, "I got a place you will love."

"Where is it?" she asks. "It's about 2 hours away from here." "I love going on long rides." She says, "It's early. Only 10 in the morning. Can you stop at my house first? I have to get something so I can look good for you."

He agrees and they stop by. She runs inside and calls Timothy and asks did they pick up her car. "Take it to my mother's house. We are going on a long ride to some place he knows of. Y'all don't leave me hanging with this guy."

"We got you. I'm sure that is the same place he probably took that little 11-year-old girl and Linda. She told me the place took some time to get there. We will see you there stall him for a few minutes if you can. I got to go get Linda." She ends the call and prepares herself for the ride.

She says, "Can we stop at the store? I would love to get something to make this more enjoyable for you."

"For me, nobody ever does anything for me. I always have to take what I want." "Well, you won't have to take anything from me because this is your day and I'm going to rock your world baby." They both laugh.

"I told you my name was Destiny and today you walked right into your Destiny."

"I like the way that sounds." He speaks. He pauses for a minute, and she asks him what's wrong.

"I'm just thinking about what I'm going to do to you," he says.

"Really," she says, " tell me what you are going to do."

"I'm going to kill you, but I'm going to rape you first." He says as he locks the doors on the cruiser so she cannot get out. She plays it cool and laughs it off.

"I like it rough, so you are talking and language now."

"Destiny, you my kind of girl, where have you been all my life?"

Before getting on the road, he has to make a stop to get some food and some drinks to have on the road, so they won't need to stop later. When he stops for the store break, she calls Timothy.

"Where y'all at this man talking about killing me he says it as a joke, but I believe he is for real. Y'all better hurry up."

"We just picked Linda up. we are on our way."

"Do y'all know where I'll be?"

"Yes, Linda says I've been there."

"Ok good! He's coming back now, and we headed to the spot."

She hangs up before he sees her on the phone. He gets back in the car Beloni doesn't know he went in there to buy some tape and rope. He puts the bag in the truck. He gets back in the car and asks Destiny if she's ready. She nods yes then he drives off.

Linda, Terrance and Timothy are on their way, but they get a flat tire. "This is going to slow us up! Come on man, let's get this tire fixed. I don't want nothing to happen to my girl!" It takes them 20 minutes to fix the tire. They are back on the road. It's 2:00 pm and they still have 2 hours to drive.

Beloni falls asleep on the way, and she feels his hand all over her. She can't blow her cover, so she says, "Wait, baby, till we get there. I got something for you." So, they continue to drive, and it's about 2:45. She looks at her watch and says, "Can you stop at a restroom? I got to go really bad." He tells her no because he didn't want anybody to see them together.

"Why not?" She says,

"For one, I'm supposed to be at work, and two, I told you what I was going to do to you; can't no one see us together."

"Are you really serious about killing me?"

"Yes," he says. "I've killed many people," laughing, "You going to meet your destiny, Destiny," he says.

"You joking, right?"

"No," he says.

"I love to rape and kill. I love to kill anyone that gets close to me." He gets this crazy look in his eyes. "Baby, I know you just playing." She doesn't want to show him that she is afraid. "Well, I like danger," she says. "Let's do this." He looks at her, smiles, and tells her she really doesn't know what she's in for. I got something for you she tells him. I got something for you, too, he says as she looks out the window. It's 3:30. They arrive at the run-down building, she says.

"I thought you were taking me to a nice place."

"No, this is my nice place. It's really nice on the inside," he says.

"Well, I got to see this," she prolongs him by looking for her shoes and purse. "Come on, for someone sees you," he yells.

She wants to call Timothy to see how far off they are, but she doesn't want to blow her cover. He says "come on" again, real loud, and she gets out of the car and walks with him to the door. He lets her in and tells her to make herself at home. He goes back to the car to get the bag he left in the trunk. At this time, she texts Timothy the word help. Timothy tells Terrance, "Man, we got to move this thing; my girl just texted me help." Linda tells them how they're only about 20 mixtures out. Timothy wants to text Beloni back, but he doesn't want to blow her cover.

Pete goes inside and sees Beloni sitting on the sofa; he asks her if she would like something to drink. She says,

"No, I would like to go to the bathroom."

"Oh, the bathroom is right over there, door number 2."

"Thanks," she says.

While in the bathroom she texts Timothy again. He responds quickly saying they're 10 minutes off. Pete knocks on the door. "Come on out, you been in there long enough," he says. When She comes out, he asks her where her cell is. "Why?"

Pete tells her, "What did I say I was going to do to you?" Laughing at her. He takes her cell and burns it. "Why did you do that?" She is really getting afraid now. "When are you going to listen to me? What have I been saying all along? Did you think I was playing? No, I'm serious as a heart attack. You are going to die today," Pete tells her. "Come," he says, "let's go sit down." They sit, Pete tells her about his childhood, about how his dad and mother would let men and women have intercourse with him at a young age. How they would sell him because neither one of them wanted to work.

Beloni says, "I can help you get through that, let me help you."

He tells her, "I would rather die than to relive my past life. Both parents are dead, I have no siblings." So, he takes off his gun holster and lays it across the chair. "Nope I'm good, now give me what I came here for." He grabs her by her hair "Oh" he says, "I thought this was a weave, this your hair Oh I'm really going to have fun with you." He pulls her down to the floor by her hair and jumps on top of her. She's trying to get her hand inside her bra to get her pocketknife, but he overpowers her. Pete says, "Wow, I like this. I got a fighter on my hand. We going to have so much fun. I enjoy fighters the most I sit back and watch them fight for their lives." He laughs really loud. Then the door bursts open, and Timothy yells. Pete tries to grab his gun; before he can get it, Linda runs and hits him with a bat knocking him out.

"That's for raping me," she says.

Terrance shoots him in the chest and says, "This one is for the little girl you raped."

They take the bat and wipe all fingerprints off it and wipe down the room and bathroom for Beloni's fingerprints. It's getting dark. They leave, and Linda says to make sure he's dead. Laurence shoots him again in the head. Check the area to see if anyone was around. They get in the car and leave. Linda tells them that my husband must never know about this. They all agree no cop like that should be on the street. "He got what he deserved; let's get something to eat. I'm hungry," Timothy says. They stopped about 2 hours up the road and heard someone talking about a cop they are looking for because they had evidence on him that will put him away for life or give him the lethal injection, a little old man says. They just listened, got their food and went and sat down to eat. At this time, it is about 7:00 pm. They get back in the car and head home. They drop Linda off first, Beloni, then Timothy. Terrance gets rid of the gun by putting it in a bucket of pure acid, letting it sit for 4 hours and tossing it in the river. There is no serial number or anything that will link them to the gun. "It's over," Terrance says. "You won't hurt anyone else."

The next day, Detective and the other office goes back out looking for Pete, Pete is nowhere to be found not even his cruiser. So, they go back to the police station and get a picture of him and ask around town if anyone seen this cop. Everyone is afraid to say anything, so everyone says no. One guy says,

"Yes, I know him, but I haven't seen him."

"How do you know him?" the cop asks.

"He is the cop that raped that 11-year-old girl. It was all over the news and they let him go." The man says.

Detective Johnson says, "yes that is true, but we have enough evidence on him to put him way for life."

"If we hear anything I'll call the police station and ask for Detective Johnson."

"Ok good," the Detective says. They leave. They stop at the Lashea's donut shop and asks if anyone seen him. The owner waited on him, but he says no one has seen him. They leave. The owner's daughter says, "He was here yesterday." "I know he was but I'm not getting into that and if you know what's good for you, you wouldn't get into it either." They continue to work.

Someone that's lives in the area where the cop police car drives by and sees the car sitting there and notice it is a different county. So, they call the police department in their county and tell them it is an out-of-town police car at one of the abandoned stores on Got Served Road.

"Ok," the officer says, "we will send someone to check it out."

At this time, it's about 10:30 am. The officer doesn't get there till 3:30 pm.

"What took you so long?" the man asks.

"I had to finish up a report for my lieutenant. It is a police car, I see. Have you seen the officer?"

"No," the man says.

"No," the man says, "that's your job." The officer goes and knocks on the door no answer. So, he turns the doorknob, and it opens right up. "OH, my God!" He gets on his radio and calls for an ambulance and the investigation unit. He goes over to him to see if he is alive, but he is not. He radios back and tells them to send the Coroner Officer. He goes back to his car and gets the yellow crime scene tape and raps it around the area. He tells the man you need to stay back and do not touch anything. The man says, "You don't have to worry about me; I'm not touching anything." The cop starts questioning the man about how long the car was there. The man tells him, "I don't know. I just saw it there and thought it was strange, so I called the police station. I would never hurt anybody. I was raised in the church, and I fear God too much to take somebody's life," he says. "Can I leave now officer? I've done my part by calling you. Here is my number just in case you need me. I have done nothing wrong. I was with my wife and kids all day yesterday."

"Ok I'll call you if I need you." The officer says.

At 4:45, the Lieutenant and the coroners' officer pull up at the same time. They walk inside and see the cop shot twice with a blow to the head, and his holster lying across the sofa. The bat there beside him. "We will take the bat in for evidence," the Lieutenant says. The Lieutenant gets on the cell and calls the other county. Detective Johnson answers the phone. The Lieutenant tells him we have one of your officers down here in our county. He has been killed he says. Detective Johnson asks, him what is the name on the badge?

"Pete Smith."

"You are kidding me, right?" Detective says.

"No, he's really here dead as a door nail."

"Can you tell me what happen?"

"No, someone driving by saw his car parked outside this abandon building and called our station, we sent someone out here and this is what they found when they opened the door."

"The AD and I will be right down."

"How long will it take you to get here?"

"About three hours. We are on our way now."

"OK, by that time we should have this wrapped up here and you can take the body and his car back with you we don't want anything to do with this case." The DA and the Detective get in their cruiser and leave the police station.

Linda walked in the door and her husband was waiting on her.

"Baby you said you was going out with your brother, but I didn't know you was going to be all day," Linda says.

"I just needed some time with my brother after everything that has happened, I'm ok now I'm good baby. Can we just lay down? I just want you to hold me."

They lay down and he asks her what they did. "We went to eat and riding," she says.

"Sounds like y'all had fun."

"Yes, we did baby." They snuggle and fall to sleep.

DA and Detective pulled up on the scene and saw his car. They ran inside and saw him in a body bag. They zipped him down to make sure it's him.

"Yep, it is Pete," the DA says.

They take all the notes the other officer had on the case, and they put him in the coroner van and took him to the morgue in their county.

"Johnson," the DA says, "we don't have to have a trial and waste the taxpayer's money. This case is closed."

"Are you sure DA."

"Yes, I'm sure. He has done so much wrong to people; he probably would have gotten the death sentence any way. So, how are we going to write this up? We will close this as no witnesses."

"Alright you the boss. Johnson says. "What if the other county brings this up? You know they have to write it up in their files."

"Johnson, I don't want you to mention this file again. Case CLOSED."

All of the officers at the station gave him a funeral service and no one showed up but the officer. DA thought what a sad way to go.

Remember what Proverbs 6:16-19 NIV says, "16 there are six things the Lord hates, seven that are detestable to him. 17 haughty eyes, a lying tongue, hands that shed innocent blood, 18 a heart that devise wicked schemes, feet that are quick to rush into evil, 19 a false witness who pours out lies and a person who stirs up conflict in the community."

So now that you have read this short story who would you say was wrong?

Why would you say they were wrong?

How would you have handled the situation?

Was Ms. Corona right for being the noise neighbor?

Was it right for Gerald to let Tracy go and not turn him over to the police officers?

Was it right for them not to tell Tracy's wife about what he did to Gerald?

Was it right for Linda, Beloni, Terrance and Timothy to keep what they did to the cop a secret from Tracy Linda's husband?

What do you think about the cop raping the little girl?

Was it right for them to kill the cop even though he did so much dirt?

Was it right for the DA and the Detective to take it on their own and not find out what happen to the bad officer Pete?

Do you think that it was sad that Pete had no family at his funeral?

Why do you think that?